*If playing as a solo, play 2nd piano part for next three measures.

Molto legato e espressivo (♩=54)

con pedale

Molto legato e espressivo (♩=54)

con pedale

12

*If playing as a solo, play 2nd piano part for next three measures.

Opt. L.H. part: **Opt. L.H. part:*

Orchestral accompaniment parts available from:
AJA Arts, 7483 Brookhaven Rd., West Bend, WI 53095